This book belongs to

_______________________________

# KiraBoo Learns Her Colours

## A KiraBoo™ Collection

Lets play with colours!

We are going to start with our Primary colours which are

**Red**, **Yellow** and **Blue**.

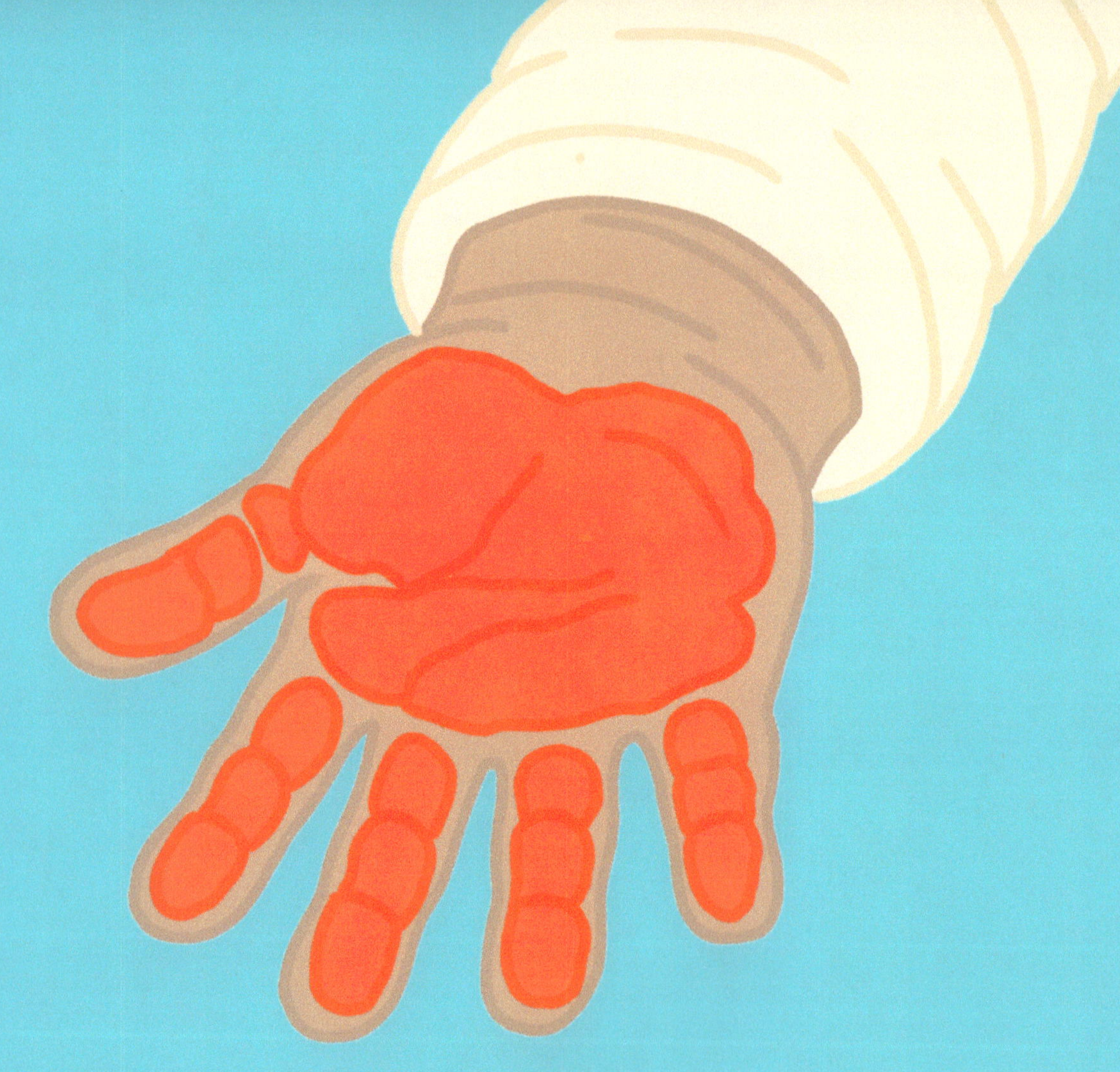

**Lets take some**

**Red**

**and**

**Yellow ...**

That makes ...

Orange!

Lets take some
Yellow

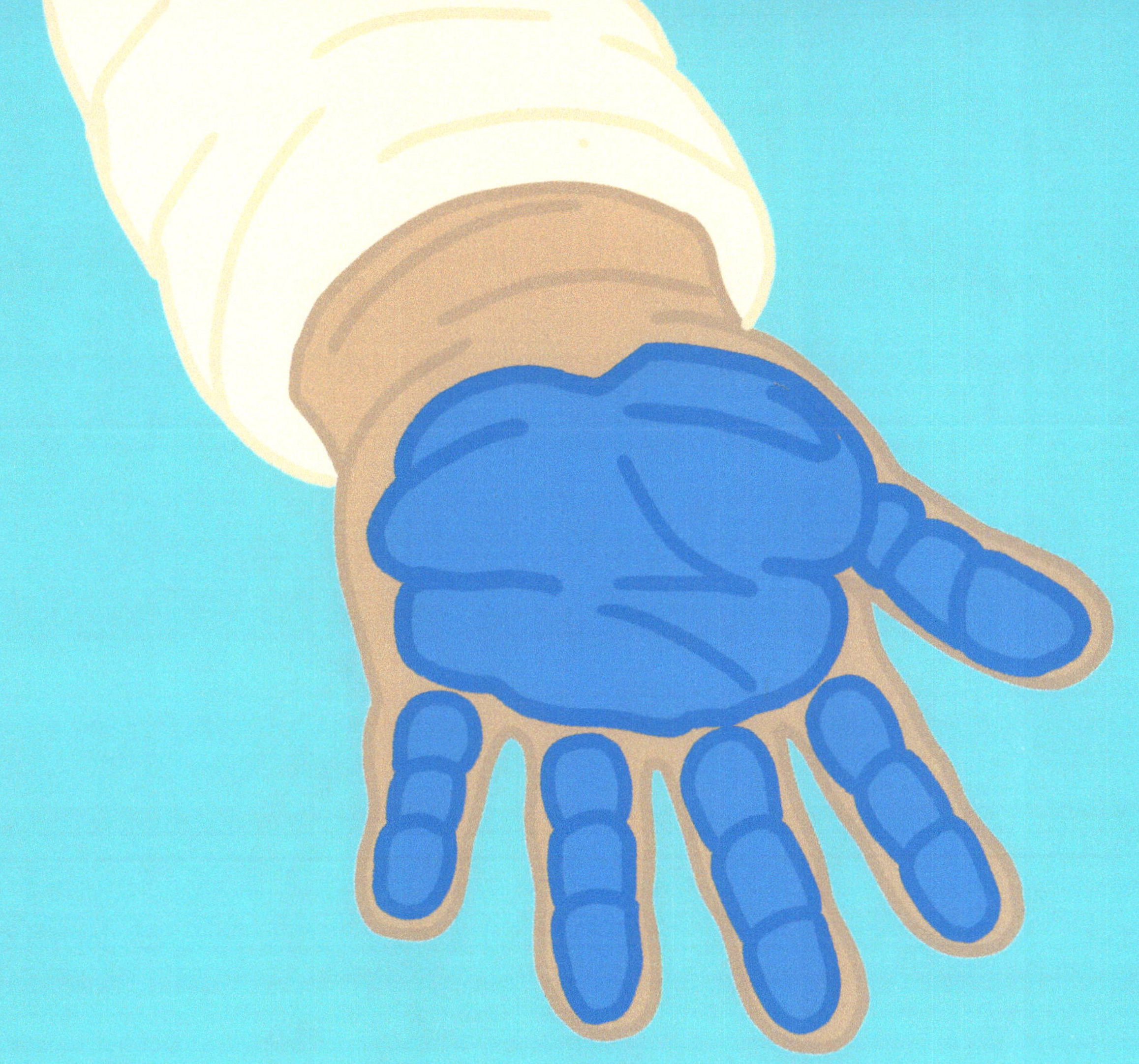

and

Blue ...

That makes ...

Green!

Lets take some

**Blue**

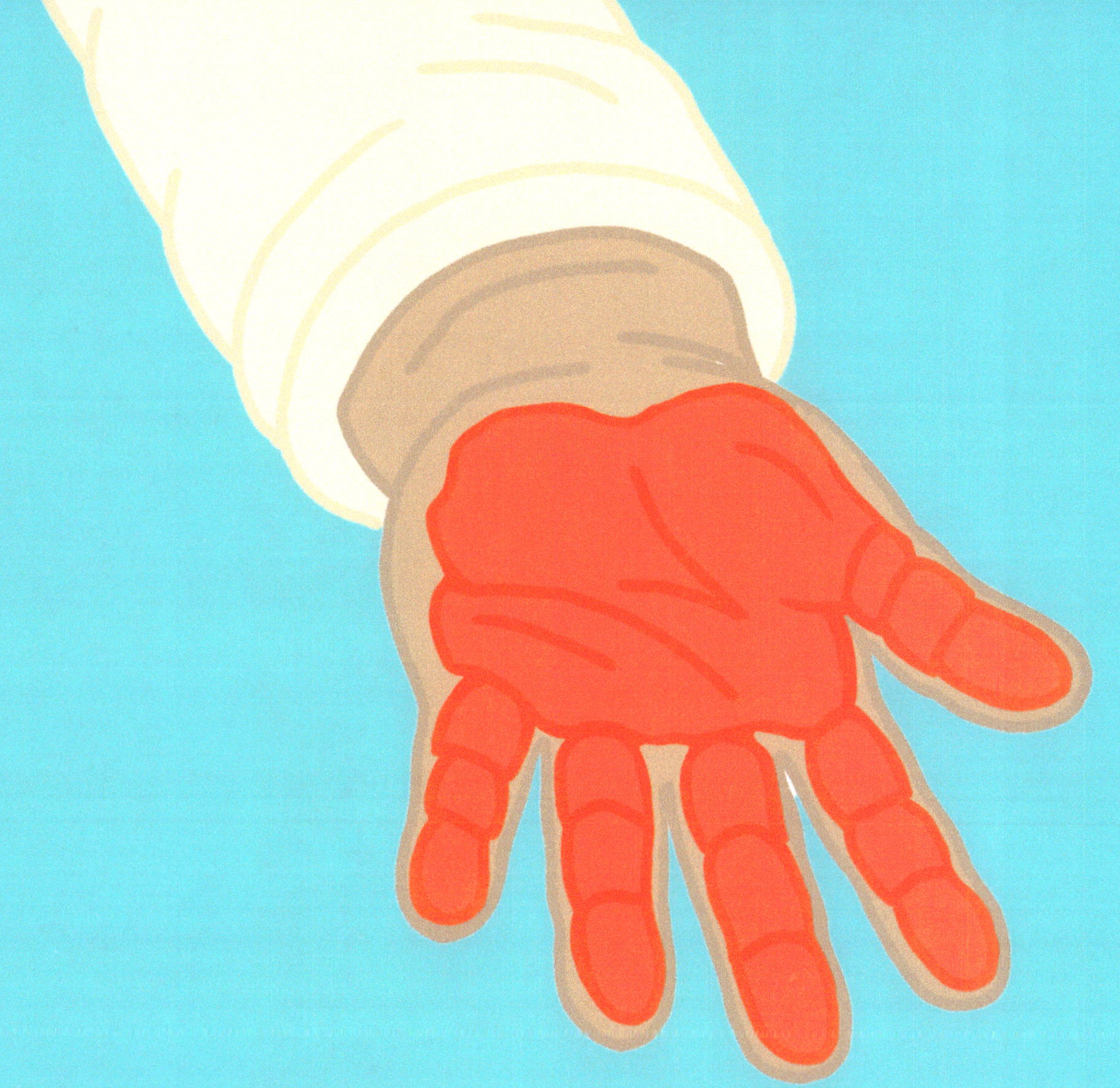

and

Red ...

# That makes ...

Purple!

Colours are
fun!

Let's go over all of the colours we just learned.

# This is Red.

# This is
# Yellow.

# This is Blue.

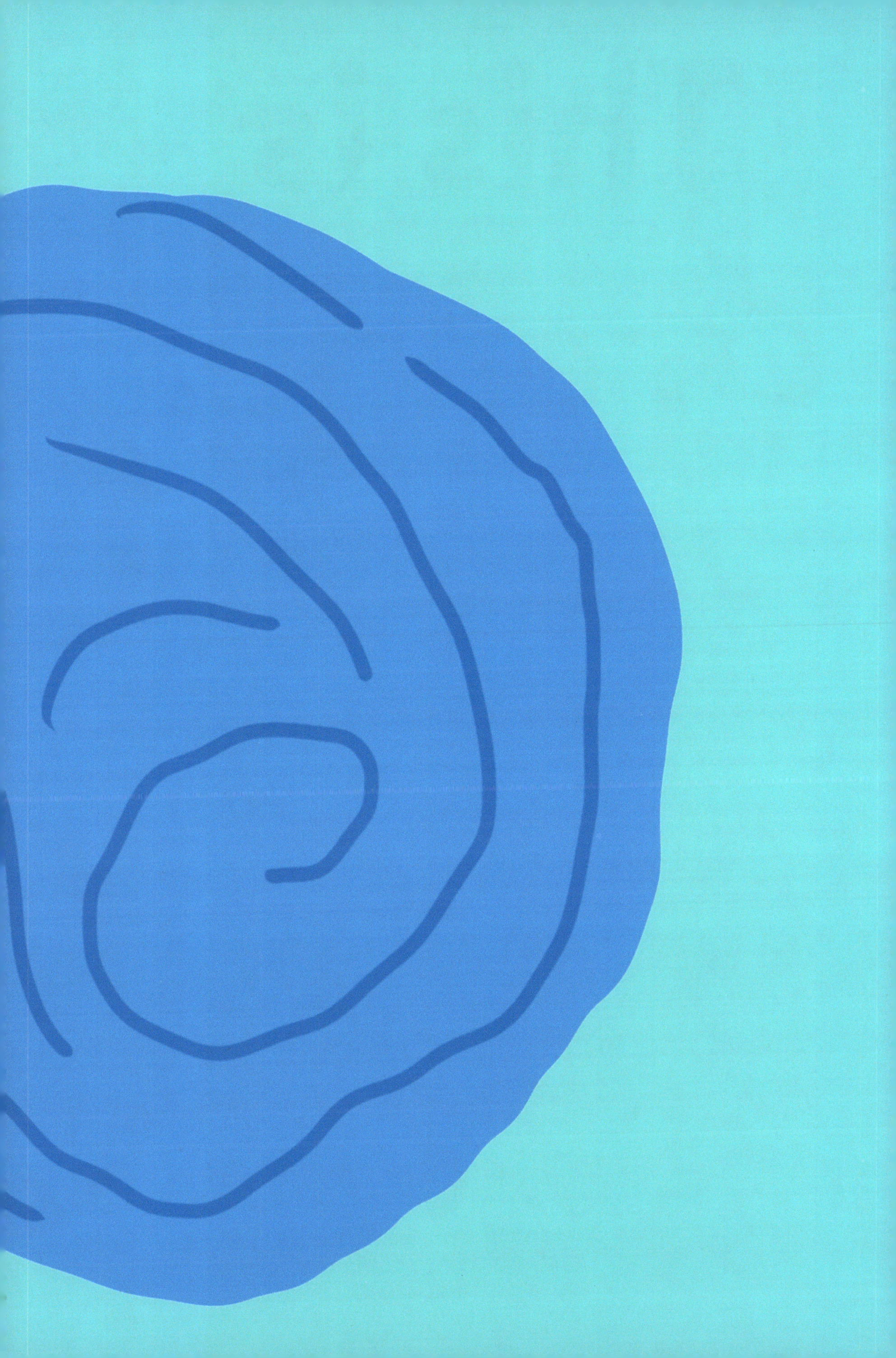

# This is Orange.

# This is Green.

# This is Purple.

Colours are
everywhere!

Can you name the colour you see?

**Little Bean Readers**

APG
PRESS